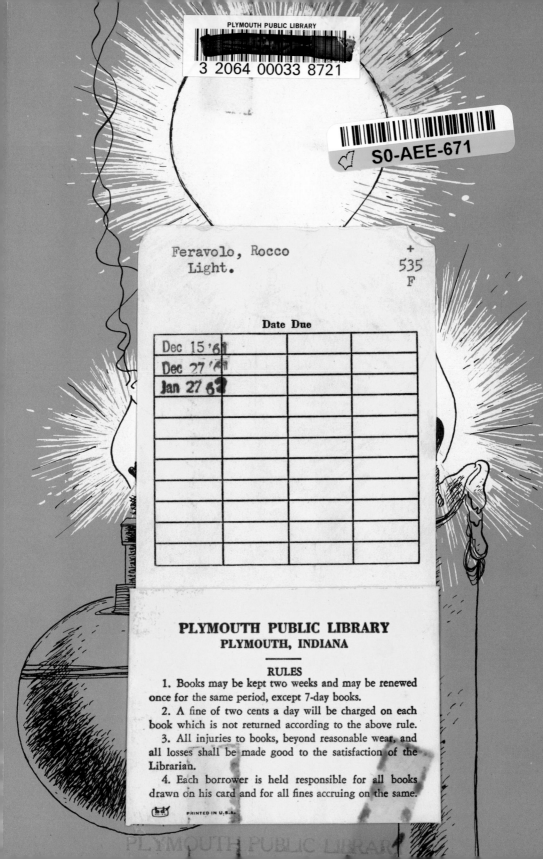

Feravolo, Rocco
Light.

+
535
F

Date Due

Dec 15 '6?		
Dec 27 '6?		
Jan 27 6?		

Junior Science Books are dedicated to all children who are eager to know more about nature and the world they live in. Written especially for young readers, each Junior Science Book has been carefully tested by the Spache Readability Formula. The purpose of this evaluation is to assure that each book can be read by primary grade children and enjoyed by young readers through the elementary grades.

Junior Science Books are edited and designed under the supervision of Nancy Larrick, Ed.D.

Junior Science Book of
LIGHT

By
Rocco V. Feravolo

Illustrated by
George Wilde

THE GARRARD PRESS
Champaign, Illinois

Contents

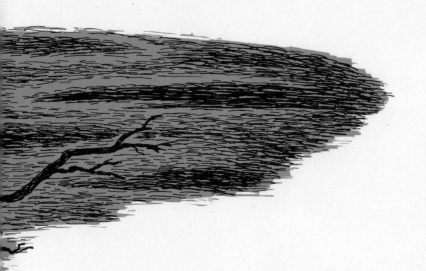

In the Beginning

Long ago, the only light came from the sun and the stars. At night the earth was dark—except when there was a moon. There were no candles, no lamps, no street lights, no neon signs.

When the sun went down, the first people went to sleep in caves or trees. When dawn came, they went forth to look for breakfast.

Finally the cave men learned how to

use fire. Where did they get fire? One Indian story is that fire came from the buffalo. When herds of buffalo galloped across the plains, their hoofs struck sparks from the rocks. The sparks set fire to the brush. Another story is that a huge panther made sparks as his claws struck stone.

Most of the early fires came from lightning. Lightning often sets fire to trees. Probably cave men took burning sticks and made their own fires. Then they had light during the dark nights. The light scared off wild animals.

Fires also warmed the caves in winter. And the cave men discovered that roasted meat is better than raw meat.

Of course there were no matches. There were no flints or steel, either. So the cave men kept their fires going day and night, year after year. In some parts of the world, that is still done.

By firelight the cave men painted pictures on the rock walls of their caves. They made simple tools of stone and bone.

Cave men had to work by firelight.

After many more years, man learned how to carry light with him. First he used torches of pine. Later he made lamps that burned candles or oil. Today we use a flashlight or the headlights of an automobile.

Now it is easy to get light anywhere. We even have electric lights in refrigerators. Baseball and football are played outdoors at night. Huge lights make the field almost like day.

Chicken houses have lights so the hens will wake up early and lay more eggs. Airplanes carry lights to prevent collisions at night.

All of us depend on light—day and night. We can't imagine living without it.

Some Objects
Make Their Own Light

The cave man got most of his light from the sun. So do we.

The sun is really a star—a huge ball of glowing gases. The sun and other stars are called *luminous objects* because they make their own light.

A burning match is a luminous object. So is a traffic light. So is a firefly.

7

Things that don't make any light are
called *non-luminous*. The moon is a non-
luminous object. It has no light of its own.
You can see the moon only because sunlight reflects from it. It's like turning a
flashlight on an owl in an oak tree at
night. You can see the owl very plainly
because your light shines on it. But the
owl is a non-luminous object, like the
moon.

Take a flashlight and a ball into a dark room. Be sure there is no light at all. Put the ball on a table. Step back. You can't see the ball because it has no light of its own. It is non-luminous.

Turn your flashlight beam on the ball. Now you can see the ball plainly. Light goes from the flashlight to the ball. Then it bounces back from the ball to your eyes. We say the light is *reflected* from the ball.

Light from the flashlight hits the ball. Then it is reflected to your eye.

The sun is like your flashlight. It shines on the moon. Like the ball, the moon has no light of its own. But it can reflect the sun's light to us. Then we can see the moon.

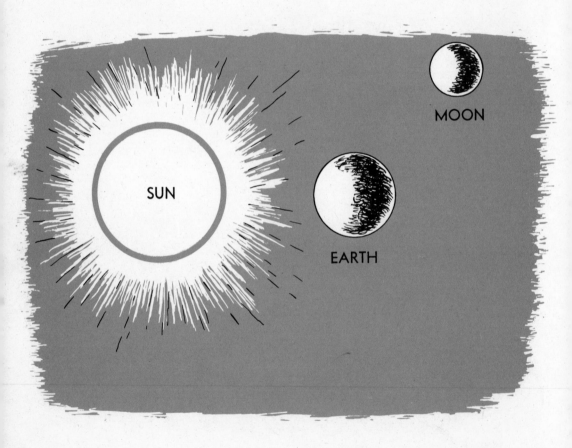

How We See

We see non-luminous things because of reflected light.

Go into a dark room and try to read this book. Of course you can't because the book has no light of its own. Turn on the light. Now you can read. The book reflects the light of the bulb to your eyes.

Lay a mirror on a table in the dark room. There should be no light in the room at all. Shine the beam of a flashlight on the mirror. Notice how the mirror reflects the light. The reflected light seems almost as bright as the beam from the flashlight.

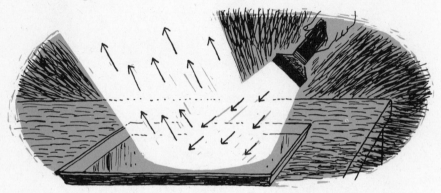

Mirror

Put a smooth piece of aluminum foil on the table. Again be sure the room is completely dark. Turn the flashlight on the foil. A lot of light will be reflected. The

Smooth foil

flat foil works almost as well as a mirror. From a smooth surface, light rays bounce back in the same direction.

Now crumple the foil into a ball. Open up the ball, but don't make the foil smooth and flat. Just lay it on the table, full of crinkles. Turn your flashlight beam on the rough foil. The light bounces off in all directions.

Crumpled foil

Rough surfaces do not reflect light as evenly as smooth surfaces.

How Light Travels

Sound can travel 1,100 feet in one second.

A rifle bullet will go three times that fast.

But light travels 186,000 miles in just one second. If a rocket ship could travel that fast, it would go around the earth seven times in a second.

Aim a strong flashlight at a tree some distance away. Press the button. The light seems to get there instantly.

Most scientists say that light is a series
of waves. The waves spread out into
space. The brighter the light, the farther
the waves travel. The light from a match
will not go far. The light from a bonfire
can be seen a long way off. The light
from the sun travels millions of miles.

Light waves are tinier than you can
imagine. Look at one inch on a ruler. In
that inch there is room for about 200,000
light waves.

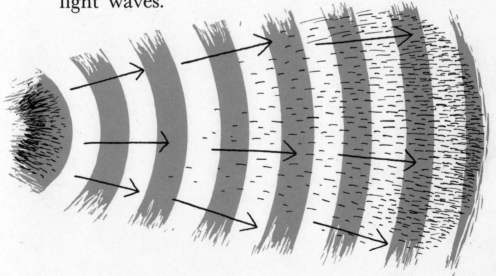

Light travels in waves like ripples on a pond.

Light travels in an almost straight line. It stops when it hits an object it can't go through. It may bounce back as reflected light.

Go into a dark room again with a flashlight. Take another person and ask him to stand away from you. Aim the flashlight at him. Hold your hand in front of the flashlight. Some light shines out from the side of your hand. But your

Your hand stops the beam of light.

friend won't be able to see the beam. Your hand has stopped it.

Now hold your hand in front of your mouth, without touching it. Say something. Your friend will hear you. The sound of your voice will go around your hand. Sound waves can turn corners.

The sound of your voice goes around your hand.

Actually, light waves can bend slightly, too. But they bend so little that only scientists can measure the bending.

Try another experiment. Take three
pieces of cardboard about 6 inches square.
Cut a hole about an inch square in each
piece. Fold over an inch at the bottom
and line up the three pieces. Use a weight
to keep each piece from falling over.
A pair of scissors, a pocket knife or a
small rock will be heavy enough.

The holes must be in a straight line.
Now put a lighted candle at one end and
look through the holes.

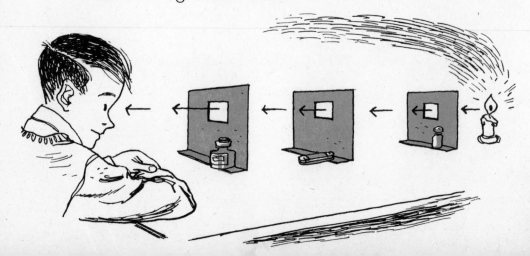

You can see the candle because the light travels in a straight line.

Now move one piece of cardboard an inch to one side. You cannot see the candle flame. Light won't turn a corner.

A Pinhole Camera

A simple pinhole camera will show that light travels in a straight line.

Cut off the top of a cereal box. Cover the hole with wax paper. You can fasten the paper with scotch tape.

With a pencil or big nail punch a hole in the bottom to make a pinhole camera.

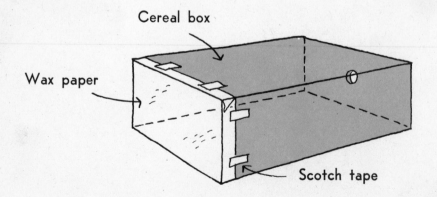

Cereal box

Wax paper

Scotch tape

Hold your camera in front of a window. You want to see the blue sky and some of the ground. Point the small hole toward the window.

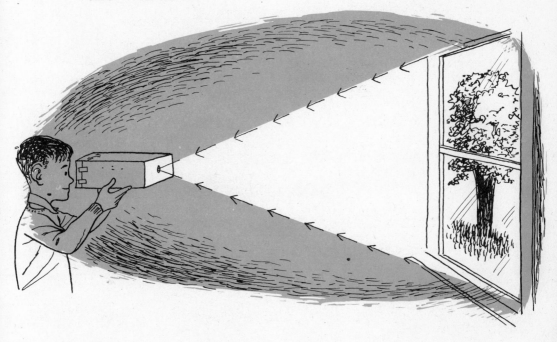

On the wax paper of your camera, the ground is at the top. The blue sky is at the bottom.

The earth and sky appear upside down because light travels in a straight line.

21

Follow the arrows in the picture below.
They show how light travels.

Suppose light rays could curve. Then
the sky would be on top as in this drawing.

But light won't bend that much. If you want the picture upright, you must tear off the bottom of the box. Then the whole picture can send its light straight to the wax paper.

A real camera is something like your pinhole camera. Pictures on the film are upside down, too.

Making a Periscope

Sometimes we want light to turn a corner. Then we use mirrors. Light hits one mirror and bounces off to another. Mirrors placed just right can bring light around a corner.

Men in a submarine use mirrors to see above water when the submarine is below water. They see with a periscope. The periscope has mirrors. You can see how it works by making a model periscope.

Get a long narrow box—the kind that wax paper comes in. You will also need two small mirrors, about 2 inches wide and 2½ inches long. They must fit inside the box.

Cut a 1-inch square on one side of the box, near the end. Turn the box over. Cut another hole on the opposite side, near the other end. Tape the mirrors inside the box as shown here.

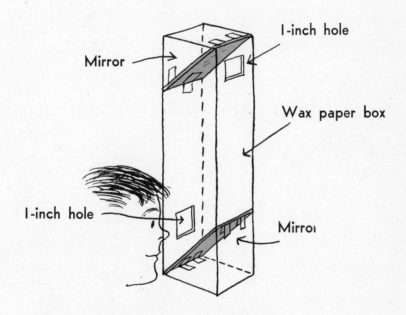

Mirror ←
1-inch hole →
Wax paper box →
1-inch hole —
Mirror ←

Now close the cover of the box. Your periscope is ready. Sit on the floor behind a tall chair. Hold the periscope so the

25

top hole sticks above the chair. You can see without being seen.

Light travels through the box from one mirror to the other. The two mirrors make it turn corners.

As another test stand behind a door that is half open. Hold your periscope out from the edge. You can see without being seen.

Things That Reflect Light

A good mirror reflects light very well. But many other objects reflect light, too. Shiny metal, jewels, water and glass are good reflectors.

Dark things reflect very little light. Go into a dark room with your flashlight, a piece of white paper and a piece of black paper.

Turn the beam on the white paper.

Hold your other hand 10 to 12 inches above the paper. Notice how much light is reflected from the paper to your hand.

Now try the same experiment with the black paper. This time little light is reflected to your hand. The black paper soaks up light as a sponge soaks up water.

On a warm day you feel hotter in a black shirt. That is because black absorbs light. But white clothes make the light rays bounce off you. You don't feel so warm.

From Transparent to Opaque

Most window glass is *transparent*. Light goes right through it.

Clear water is transparent, too. You can look into shallow water and see a fish looking at you. Or you might see a snapping turtle snapping up a tadpole.

Many plastics are also transparent. You can see the cookies or peanuts inside a plastic bag.

Some things let a little light pass through. But they don't give a clear view.

The frosted glass on a bathroom window is an example. So is the wax paper around a sandwich. These things are *translucent*.

Most things won't let any light pass through them. A brick wall is a good example. You can think of many others: a tin can, a door, a heavy coat. All of these things are *opaque*.

This page is also opaque. Thick paper is generally more opaque than thin paper.

A printer tests different papers for opaqueness. You can do the same. Get a piece of writing paper, a piece of tissue paper and a piece of drawing paper. Put your samples side by side over clear black type. A big calendar will do very well. Now see which piece of paper hides the printing best. That one is more opaque than the others.

Shadows

When light hits an opaque object, it stops. That's how shadows are formed. Sunlight won't go through your body, for example. Some morning stand with your back to the sun. You will see your shadow on the ground before you. That is where your body stopped the sunlight.

In the middle of the day your own shadow is very short. The sun shines down on you. There isn't much of an angle.

In the early morning and the late afternoon, your shadow is much longer. The light from the sun hits you at an angle. Your shadow looks like the shadow of a giant.

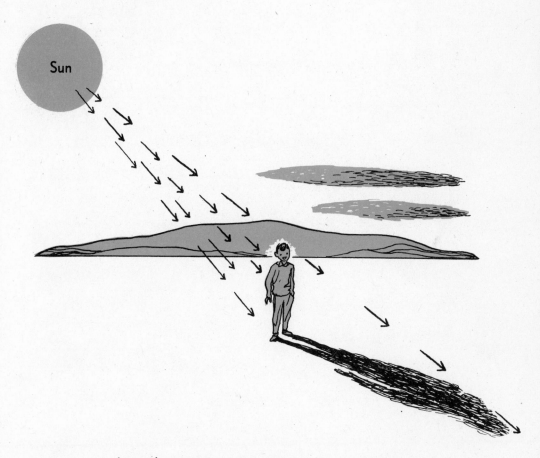

In early morning your shadow is much longer.

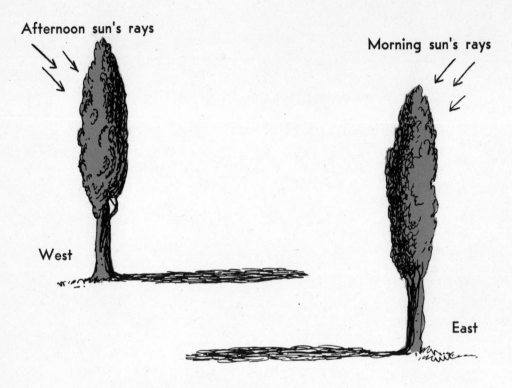

Afternoon sun's rays

Morning sun's rays

West

East

The shadow moves as the sun moves.

Sunlight won't go through the thick branches of a tree. So there is shade or shadow under the tree. The shadow moves as the sun moves.

The shaded place under a tree isn't as dark as night. It gets some light. You can see very well under a tree.

The reason is that light rays are

34

scattered every which way. They are reflected by things on the ground and in the air. A concrete sidewalk reflects light rays. Tiny particles of dust in the air reflect light, too. Houses, leaves, stones and almost anything will reflect some light.

The walls inside your house reflect light. When the sun shines, every room has light. The light is spread all around the room.

The shadow on the sundial tells the time.

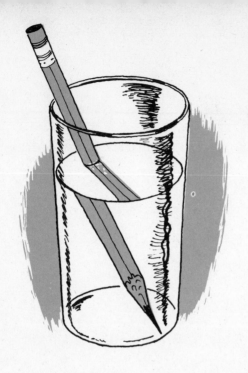

Light Rays Can Bend

When you walk through water a foot deep, you have trouble. The water slows your feet and legs.

Water slows light rays, too. You can see what happens.

Fill a glass about two-thirds full of water. Put a pencil in the glass.

The pencil looks slightly bent at the top of the water. Of course it really isn't bent. The bending is in the light rays. This bending is *refraction* of light. It happens when light goes through transparent things like water and glass and air.

Light rays bend when they come to water. They bend because water slows them down.

Light goes through space at 186,000 miles a second. It goes through water at 139,000 miles a second. It goes through

Light rays bend when they come to water.

glass at 124,000 miles. And it is still slower when it shines through a diamond.

This experiment will show how light bends. Spread some salt on a level part of the sink. It should make a smooth patch about ¼ inch high. (You can also use the kitchen table. But keep salt off the floor, where it can cause trouble.) Roll a round pencil toward the salt. Let the sharp end come to the salt first.

Salt

Notice what happens. As the sharp end rolls onto the salt, it slows down. But the other end keeps rolling at the same speed on the smooth surface. It goes faster than the sharp end. And so the pencil makes a small turn.

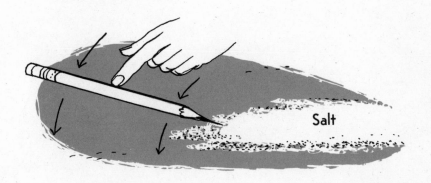

Salt

When light goes from air into water, it behaves like the pencil. The first light rays to strike the water slow down. This makes them bend, just as the pencil bends its path when it comes to the salt.

Another experiment will show that water bends light rays. Put a penny in an aluminum pie plate. Put the pie plate on the sink or a table. Step back about 4 feet or until the coin disappears.

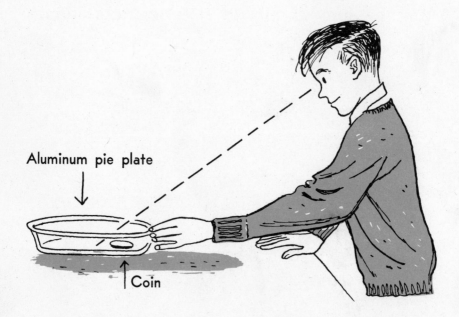

Aluminum pie plate

Coin

Have someone pour water into the pie plate slowly. Soon you can see the coin.

Where coin appears to be

Coin

It seems to have moved. Of course it is still in the same place. You can see it because water bends the light rays. The same thing happened with the pencil in the glass of water.

Lenses

Ancient people had no eye glasses or telescopes. They had no magnifying glasses. They had no microscopes. They had to depend on their eyes alone.

Their wise men studied the stars and moon. But they could see no more than you can when you step outdoors.

Then, about 700 years ago, eye glasses were invented. Nobody knows exactly when or how. People with weak eyes could see better through eye glasses. The curved pieces of glass made everything look bigger. They magnified things.

Each curved piece of glass is a *lens*. Lens is the Latin word for a kind of seed. It is curved somewhat like a glass lens.

If you have a flat piece of glass, light passes straight through it. That is why window glass lets you see things as they are. It works like this:

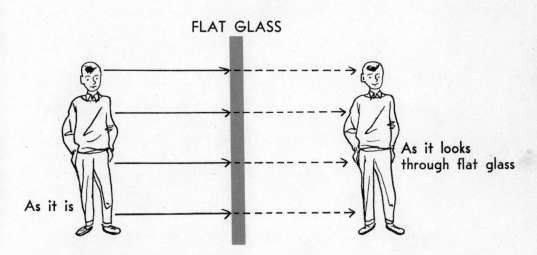

FLAT GLASS

As it is

As it looks through flat glass

A curved piece of glass, or lens, can bend light rays.

There are two main kinds of lenses. A *concave* lens is thicker at the edges than in the center. It can make things look smaller than they really are.

CONCAVE LENS

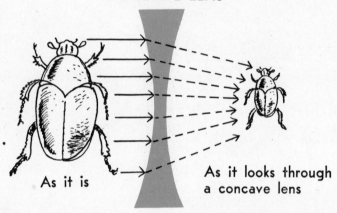

As it is

As it looks through a concave lens

But sometimes you want to see things larger than they really are. Or you want to see far-away things as though they were close up. For this you need a *convex* lens.

A convex lens is thicker in the middle than at the edges. It can bend rays of light to make things look bigger.

44

CONVEX LENS

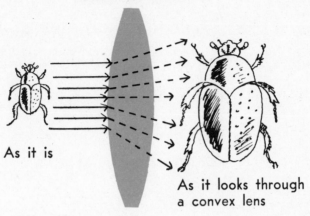

As it is

As it looks through
a convex lens

A magnifying glass is a convex lens. It is used to make things look larger.

Hold a magnifying glass over a postage stamp. You will see fine lines you never noticed before. The convex lens has made the stamp look bigger.

Take a newspaper outdoors when the sun is shining. You will see how a magnifying glass bends the light rays.

Place the newspaper in the bright sunlight. Hold the magnifying glass a few inches above it. Place it so the sun's rays fall directly on the glass.

Move the glass up and down until you get a hot spot on the paper. Then hold the glass steady. The paper will begin to smoke. Finally it will begin to burn.

The paper burns because the magnifying glass bends many of the sun's rays. It brings them together at the same spot. That spot gets very hot indeed.

A Dark Box
for Light Experiments

You can learn more about light rays if you make a dark box. Get a carton about 24 inches long, 12 inches wide and 12 inches high. A much bigger carton can be cut down to the right size.

Cut an opening in the front about 18 inches long and 8 inches high. Cover this with a large piece of blue cellophane. (You can buy blue cellophane at art

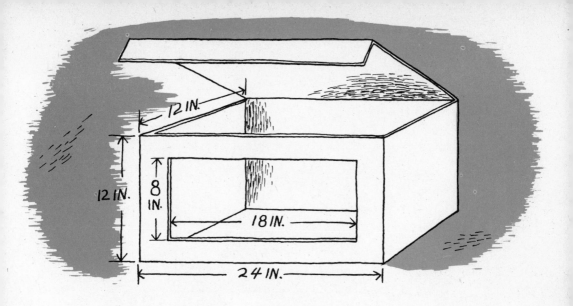

stores and many 5-and-10 cent stores.)

In one end, punch two holes with a pencil. One should be above the other. They should be about one inch apart.

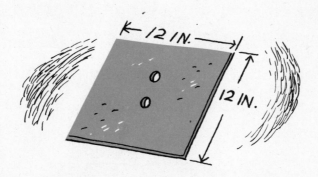

Paint the inside of the box black.

Your dark box will show how the magnifying glass bends light rays. Stand the magnifying glass straight up in the middle of the box. Use clay to hold the handle. (Or you can take a block of wood and bore a hole for the handle.)

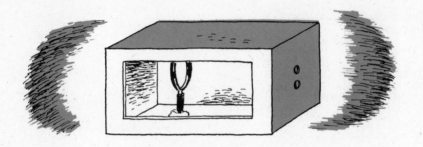

Get some incense from a novelty store. Any kind will do—all you need is smoke. Smoke makes the light easier to see.

Light the incense and put it in the box, behind the magnifying glass.

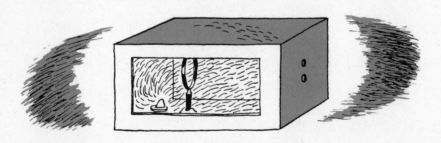

Now aim your flashlight at the two holes in the end of the box.

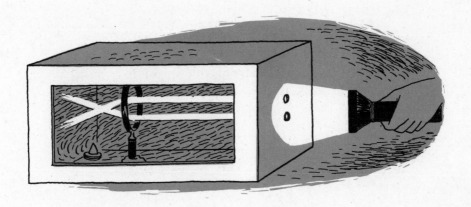

The two beams of light cross after they go through the magnifying glass.

Then the beams spread out. The bottom beam becomes the top beam. The top beam goes to the bottom. And that's why a pinhole camera makes objects appear upside down.

Your magnifying glass can show you an upside-down picture in daylight.

Stand with your back to a window. Hold the magnifying glass in your right hand, to one side. Don't try to look through it.

Hold a piece of white paper in your left hand. Make sure that light from the window goes through the magnifying glass and falls on the paper.

Move the magnifying glass back and forth. Finally you will get a clear image on the paper. The view from the window will be upside down—just like the light beams in your dark box.

And it will be much smaller even though you use a convex lens.

Colors in Light

A rainbow is a beautiful sight. You are likely to see one when rain falls while the sun shines. It comes from sunlight passing through raindrops.

Sometimes you can see the colors of a rainbow inside your house. There will be a small patch of color on a wall or table. It comes from sunlight passing through water in a glass.

You can make a rainbow outdoors with the garden hose. Stand sideways to the sun. Make a very fine spray with the hose. The sun's rays will give you a small rainbow.

You can get a closer look at rainbow colors with a glass prism. A prism like this may be bought for about a dollar in most stores that sell toys.

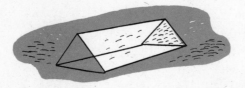

Hold your prism near a window. Turn it slowly in the sunlight. You will see the colors of the rainbow on the floor or wall. These are the colors:

Red   Orange   Yellow   Green
Blue   Indigo   Violet

The three primary colors in paints are red, yellow and blue. Mix red and yellow paint, and you get orange. Mix blue and yellow and you have green.

In light, the three primary colors are red, green and blue. You get the colors of the rainbow by mixing these three.

Take two flashlights and colored cellophane for an experiment with the colors in light. Cover the lens of one flashlight with red cellophane. Cover the other flashlight with green cellophane.

Shine the two flashlights on a sheet of white paper in a dark room. The paper will look yellow.

Light Is Life

Every living thing depends on sunlight.
Without sunlight, there could be no
grass, no vegetables, no trees. There could
be no animals that live on plants. There
could be no animals that eat the animals
that live on plants.

Even creatures that live in the dark
depend on sunlight. Consider termites.
They eat wood from the inside of timbers
and logs. They avoid daylight. But with-

out sunlight, there would be no trees for the termites to eat.

Sunlight provides us with clothing of cotton and wool. It provides us with shoes of leather. It makes roses bloom in our gardens, and cattails bloom in the swamp.

Sunlight from millions of years ago makes automobiles run. It makes electric lights shine, too. How? Because gasoline comes from oil. Oil was formed by rotting

plants when the earth was younger. Most power plants make electricity by burning coal. And coal comes from plants of long ago. The coal fire heats water into steam. The steam turns the dynamos that make electricity.

When you read a book by electric light, remember that ancient sunlight makes the electric light shine.

Index

ABOUT THE AUTHOR

ROCCO V. FERAVOLO, elementary school principal and Science Chairman of the Public Schools of Morristown, N. J., received the Science Teacher Achievement Recognition Award in 1957. His project: "Elementary Astronautics for the Gifted Child in Science."

Mr. Feravolo is a graduate of Montclair State College and has completed a year of postgraduate work at Rutgers University. For the past three years he has been an instructor of science in the Extension Division of Newark State College. In most of his classes he has used new workshop techniques developed to help teachers gain greater assurance in their science teaching. In this connection, he has designed many gadgets and audio-visual aids by which teachers can present scientific concepts in more dramatic and meaningful ways.

As a recreational side line, he coaches fencing at Drew University in Madison, N. J.

ABOUT THE ARTIST

GEORGE WILDE was born in Darby, Pennsylvania, and studied at the Philadelphia Museum School of Art and the Pennsylvania Academy of Fine Arts. The next two years he spent in Europe on Cresson Traveling Scholarships awarded for his outstanding art work.

Since 1952, Mr. Wilde has given full time to book illustration. *All About the Atom* and *All About the Wonders of Chemistry* are among the many books he has illustrated.

His wife, Irma Wilde, is also a well-known illustrator of children's books. Their daughter, who studied at Philadelphia Museum School of Art, is also a free-lance artist. The Wildes live in Philadelphia.

62